Adelaide

Steve Parish • *Australia from the Heart*

Contents

ADELAIDE FROM THE HEART

Adelaide, known as the "Festival City", is a fitting capital for South Australia – the fourth largest of the nation's States and territories. Once a small, pleasantly rural city, Adelaide has matured into a sophisticated centre for culture and the arts, and annually hosts some of Australia's most popular festivals.

Arcing around the capital, from Mount Gambier in the south-east to the Nullarbor in the west, are diverse natural environments. The State is blessed with more than 3700 kilometres of scenic coastline, with desert inland and fertile soils in its south-east.

Among the many natural and human-created fascinations of the State, most within easy reach of Adelaide, are the viticultural regions, the heritage towns in the Adelaide Hills, seaside towns such as Victor Harbor, and the wild beauty of Kangaroo Island. It is this variety of landscapes and leisure activities that gives South Australia a special place in my heart.

Steve Parish

An aerial view of Adelaide city and the Torrens River with the Festival Centre and Convention Centre at centre and Adelaide Oval at bottom right.

The City

A GRACEFUL AND PLANNED CITY

For more than 13,000 years the land on which Adelaide is built was home to the Kaurna Aboriginal people, until 1836 when Governor John Hindmarsh and some 170 free settlers docked at Holdfast Bay, Glenelg, in the HMS Buffalo. *However, unlike most Australian capitals, Adelaide was not built on the back of convict labour, but was Australia's first example of true colonisation. Colonel William Light, the Surveyor-General, carefully planned the city around the Torrens River and a central grid bordered by parklands, making today's Adelaide a spacious and easily-navigated city. Surrounding land was sold to free settlers and migrants, artisans, skilled workers and farmers, mostly from Europe and the United Kingdom.*

The Mitchell Building, University of Adelaide, North Terrace.

The World War I memorial in Pennington Gardens, with St Peter's Cathedral beyond.

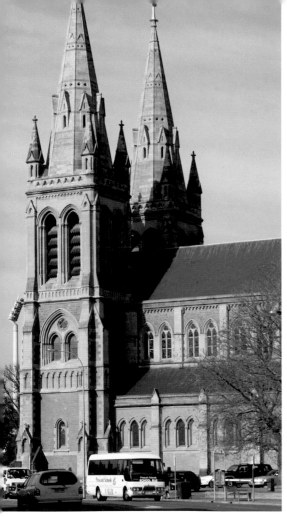

Grand churches, such as St Peter's Cathedral, grace the skyline.

Parliament House, opened in 1889, was built with Kapunda marble and West Island granite.

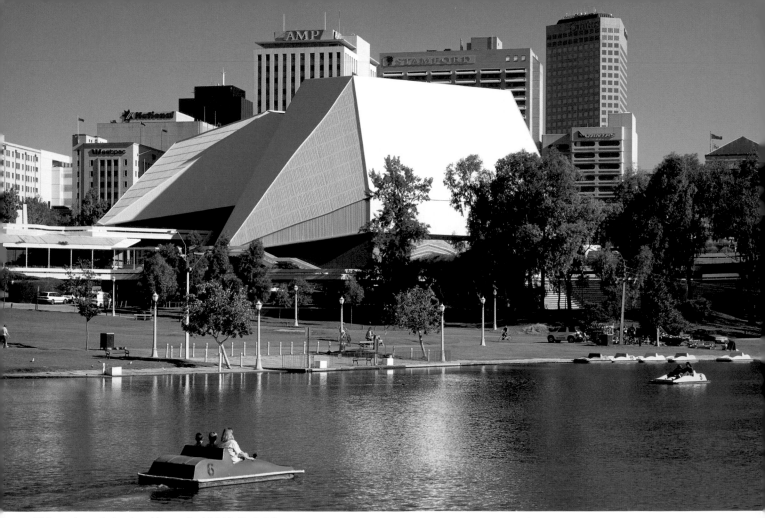

Visitors take a relaxing river ride past the Adelaide Festival Centre.

On Torrens Lake, the excursion launch *Popeye* passes the Festival Centre.

The River Torrens, crossed by Adelaide Bridge, is at the heart of the city.

Cycling along the riverside paths is a popular way to travel.

Top to bottom: Strolling along North Terrace; rowers pass the Rotunda in Elder Park.

ART, OLD AND NEW

The city streets are adorned with public art in an exciting variety of styles – cutting-edge modern, stately sculpture, and traditional and modern Aboriginal designs. Adelaide City Council's Aboriginal Studies Trail provides an insight into the art and culture of the State's Indigenous people.

Indigenous artwork *Yerrakartarta* on the forecourt of the Hyatt Hotel at North Terrace.

Cityscape by Otto Hajek covers the southern plaza of the Festival Centre.

Above, left to right: The South African War Memorial on the corner of North Terrace and King William Street; a student, a farmer and a young girl watched over by an armed angel representing the Spirit of Duty, are depicted in the The National Soldiers' Memorial, on the corner of North Terrace and Kintore Avenue.

W.J. Maxwell's sculpture of Scots poet Robert **Burns** was unveiled in 1894.

A female figure looks down from the plinth of the statue of King Edward VII.

Spheres by Bert Flugelman is a rendezvous point.

The East End of the city is a thriving dining and shopping precinct.

18

Marguerite Derricourt's bronze pig sculptures delight.

CITY ON THE GO

Adelaide is one of Australia's friendliest cities and its residents enjoy a laid-back lifestyle manifested in a cruisy city culture. The well-planned, compact CBD makes it easy to dine with friends, stroll the streets, the mall or the riverbanks, watch street performers or parades and visit shops, museums or galleries.

The city is also a multicultural metropolis, honouring both its Indigenous and immigrant heritage. In keeping with this celebration of cultural diversity is South Australia's reputation as the "Festival State", with alternative events, such as the Fringe Festival and WOMADelaide world music and dance festival, drawing artists, performers and audiences from around the world.

Above: A busker entertains shoppers and passers-by in Rundle Mall.

Left: Adelaide has more restaurants per person than any Australian city, with enough variety to suit all tastes.

From coffee to cuisine, Adelaide's Rundle Mall and the East End offer numerous dining options.

A cornucopia of colourful produce at the Central Market.

Students, visitors and locals will marvel at the many exhibits on display in the South Australian Museum.

Top to bottom: Inside the foyer of the Museum; the Museum at night.

The South Australian Museum, on tree-lined North Terrace, is one of Australia's most-visited cultural institutions. It boasts over six levels of exhibits, including the world's most extensive collection of Aboriginal culture, with more than 3000 Indigenous artefacts, as well as Pacific collections and an Ancient Egyptian room.

It is also a significant centre for South Australian natural history, displaying a fascinating array of opalised fossils in the Origin Energy Fossil Gallery. Outside, manicured lawns and pleasant parks and gardens add to its popularity.

The Gardens

NATURE FOR ALL

Inside the Botanic Gardens' ornate main gates, which were imported from England in 1880, are more than 20 hectares of botanic beauty. The gardens were part of Colonel Light's vision for the city, but were not formally established until 1857. Fountains, lakes, an intricately designed 19th-century Palm House and the diversity of flora make the gardens a wonderful place to while away an afternoon. North of the gardens is the shady Botanic Park, which attracts picnickers and birdwatchers on weekends.

Top left: Boy and Serpent fountain. **Above:** The Palm House, imported from Germany in 1875.

Queensland Moreton Bay fig trees grow in Botanic Park.

Clockwise from top left: King of the Jungle, the Lion; Waterbuck; the Hamadryas Baboon was the sacred baboon of the ancient Egyptians and often featured on their temples and ornaments; a Zebra roams the Africa exhibit; Hippopotamuses loll and wallow in the zoo's Nile Hippopotamus House.

ADELAIDE ZOO & MONARTO

Adelaide Zoo, opened in 1883, is Australia's second-oldest zoo and its many preserved 19th-century buildings make it one of the most attractive. The zoo takes care of more than 3400 animals, both native and exotic, with its major exhibits being a South-East Asian Rainforest; a reconstruction of Seal Bay on Kangaroo Island; the Australian Rainforest Wetlands walk-through aviary, the Nocturnal House, and the Reptile House.

Just a short drive from Adelaide, towards Murray Bridge, is Monarto Zoological Park, where African animals roam the plains in open enclosures. This 1000-hectare sanctuary began in 1983 as a special purpose breeding facility and still plays a major role in species conservation.

after dark

ADELAIDE AFTER DARK

Adelaide is at its most spectacular at night when the city's many fountains and the facades of historic buildings are illuminated by lights of varying hues, creating a wash of colour throughout the streets. Numerous cafés, clubs, and restaurants, as well as the casino in the heritage-listed Railway Station, come alive with patrons. Even the mirrored surface of the Torrens reflects the city's twilight joie de vivre.

Clockwise from top left: The city streets light up at sunset; Railway Station and Casino; John Dowie's fountain *The Three Rivers* in Victoria Square.

Port Adelaide

A MARITIME MARVEL

Port Adelaide, once known as Port Misery due to the mud and mosquitos, preserves South Australia's engaging sea-faring history. Wander through heritage-listed buildings, the Maritime Museum, National Railway Museum or the historic lighthouse at Queen's Wharf.

Above: Port Adelaide from the air.
Opposite, left to right: The Maritime Museum; the historic lighthouse at Queen's Wharf was first lit in 1869.

Above and right: Glenelg Jetty stretches into Gulf St Vincent.

THE BEACH

Glenelg, on Holdfast Bay, was the site of the proclamation of South Australia as a province, a fact commemorated each year on 28 December, which the South Australians call "Proclamation Day". With white sand lapped by the calm waters of Gulf St Vincent, Glenelg is also regarded as one of the State's finest beaches. Strolling along the jetty, or dropping a line over the side, are common pastimes in this relaxed suburb. Once the sun sets, numerous alfresco dining venues lure customers in for a drink or a meal by the beach.

Looking from Glenelg Jetty over the city to the Adelaide Hills.

Clockwise from top: Café culture; St Peter's Anglican Church, dating from 1883; the Glenelg Tram, Adelaide's last; alfresco venues abound.

A replica of *HMS Buffalo* anchored at Patawalonga Boat Haven houses a restaurant and museum.

Above: There are stunning views from the lookout.
Right: Artists re-create the beauty of the hills.

HEAD FOR THE HILLS

Just a short drive from the city leads to several quaint towns nestled in the lush folds of the Adelaide Hills, many with a distinctly Teutonic flavour, such as historic Hahndorf. Mount Lofty, the most easily recognised peak in the hills, is a popular lookout for visitors, affording excellent views of the city and its surrounds. Nearby, wander through the lakeside gardens at Mount Lofty Botanic Gardens or learn more about native wildlife at Cleland Wildlife Park.

Western Grey Kangaroos at Cleland Wildlife Park.

Streets, shops and houses in Hahndorf hark back to 1830s Prussia and Germany.

Plump sheep and sturdy vines flourish in the Adelaide Hills.

Tanunda, in the centre of the Valley, is encircled by farmlands and verdant vineyards.

Looking across the vineyards to the Barossa Range, with Little Kaiser Stuhl and Kaiser Stuhl at centre.

Wine Country

BAROSSA VALLEY & CLARE VALLEY

Some of Australia's best wines are produced in South Australia, with Barossa Valley, Clare Valley, Coonawarra, McLaren Vale and Langhorne Creek all producing vintages of world-renowned quality. But with historic chateaus, charming towns and rustic cottages set among vine-covered hills, the landscapes are often as appealing as the tipple. Hundreds of thousands of visitors per year flock to South Australia's wine-growing regions to pleasure their palates with wines straight from the cellar door.

A truck laden with barrels on route to a winery.

Fields in the foothills of the Barossa Range are clothed in green and purple.

THE PENINSULAS

FLEURIEU, YORKE & EYRE PENINSULAS

South Australia juts into the waters of the Southern Ocean in three jagged peninsulas – Fleurieu, Yorke and Eyre – separated by Gulf St Vincent and the Spencer Gulf. On the eastern shores of Fleurieu Peninsula are charming Victor Harbor and other seaside holiday towns; on the western shores, beaches sweep north to Adelaide. At the very tip of the Yorke Peninsula, Innes National Park attracts surfers, anglers, bushwalkers, conservationists and birdwatchers. Further north, golden fields of wheat and barley grow in soil that was once rich with minerals in the State's "copper triangle". The Eyre Peninsula, named after Edward John Eyre who explored from Port Lincoln to Fowlers Bay in 1840, comprises reserves, national parks, bushland and the vast plains of the Nullarbor, north of the Great Australian Bight. In the south is prime sheep and wheat farming land, but the region is also renowned for its thriving seafood industry.

The Cape Spencer Lighthouse, Yorke Peninsula, with Althorpe Island in the background.

A winding country road near Bute paints a typical Yorke Peninsula rural scene.

Morning light touches the beach at Lincoln National Park on the Eyre Peninsula.

An aerial view of Port Noarlunga, on the western coast of the Fleurieu Peninsula, and its jetty.

Vignerons around McLaren Vale, Fleurieu Peninsula, have created fine wines since the 1870s.

Ordered rows of vines in leaf.

The Harbor

Just a one hour drive from Adelaide is pretty Victor Harbor, once a leading port for Murray River trade and now a major tourist destination. Settled in 1837 as a whaling port, Victor Harbor was once considered a possible site for South Australia's capital city. History buffs can explore the old-fashioned charm of the region on the SteamRanger Cockle Train, which runs along Encounter Bay to Goolwa, or with a ride to nearby Granite Island on Australia's only horse-drawn tram. Nature lovers also flock to Victor Harbor to see nesting Little Penguins, and migrating Southern Right Whales in spring.

Patient Clydesdales carry visitors by tram from Victor Harbor to Granite Island.

Clockwise from top: Southern Right Whales visit Victor Harbor in spring; an old-style streetscape in the township; Granite Island, seen behind Victor Harbor.

Kangaroo Island

Australia's third-largest island, situated in the Southern Ocean just off the Fleurieu Peninsula, was first explored by Europeans in 1802, when Matthew Flinders climbed what is now called Prospect Hill and sighted mainland South Australia.

Among Kangaroo Islands attractions are the local gourmet produce, pretty towns, good fishing, and natural beauties such as the magnificent coastal rock formations of Admiral's Arch and Remarkable Rocks. Wildlife to be found in the numerous conservation parks includes Australian Pelicans and Little Penguins, New Zealand Fur-seals at Cape du Couedic, Australian Sea-lions at Seal Bay Conservation Park and Western Grey Kangaroos, from which the island takes its name.

Cape Willoughby Lighthouse, Kangaroo Island.

Top to bottom: Pennington Bay, on the south-eastern side of Kangaroo Island; the clear blue waters of Vivonne Bay, between Capes Gantheaume and Kersaint.

Admirals Arch at Cape du Couedic in the island's south-west.

Clockwise from above: The pits and melon holes weathered in the granite of the Remarkable Rocks; an Osprey returns to its nest; Western Grey Kangaroo.

The Outback

Almost eighty percent of the State is taken up by the South Australian Outback. Mining ushered in a brief period of prosperity in the 1850s and 1880s, but now the Outback is littered with abandoned stations, historical ruins and virtual ghost towns, defeated by the elements and isolation. Most modern towns rely heavily on tourism. The rugged beauty of the Flinders Ranges dominates the Outback landscape from the Spencer Gulf north to the edge of the Strzelecki Desert. Gorges, lookouts, bluffs and the amazing Wilpena Pound tower above dry plains dotted sparsely with gum trees. This ancient, barren landscape preserves significant Aboriginal art sites of the Adnyamathanha people.

The desolate Flinders Ranges.

Delicate Ptilotus flowers contrast with the harsh backdrop of the Painted Desert.

Wilpena Pound, a natural amphitheatre with stone walls of up to 500 metres in height, stretches over 90 square kilometres.

Australia's hardy plants and animals have developed specially adapted traits to save water and energy in the dry conditions.

Left to right: The river passes rugged sandstone cliffs at Walker Flat; picnicking beside the *PS Murray Princess*; paddlewheelers still ply the Murray, taking holiday-makers for a leisurely trip back in time.

The Murray

AUSTRALIA'S LONGEST RIVER

South Australia's arable land is watered by Australia's longest river. "Old Man Murray" winds 650 kilometres through the State, passing deep valleys, stands of river red gum, citrus groves and vineyards, before reaching Lake Alexandrina. Paddlewheelers, steamers and barges plied the river until the 1890s, carrying cargoes of wheat, timber, and wool. Many larger towns, such as Morgan and Mannum, preserve historical sites from the era when the river was the major source of trade. When a rail system was established, river trade declined, but irrigation enabled fruit growing and farming along the river's banks, making the riverlands the fruit bowl of the State.

From an early age, Steve Parish has been driven by his undying passion for Australia to photograph every aspect of it, from its wild animals and plants to its many wild places. Then he began to turn his camera on Australians and their ways of life. This body of work forms one of Australia's most diverse photographic libraries. Over the years, these images of Australia have been used in thousands of publications, from cards, calendars and stationery to books – pictorial, reference, guide and children's. Steve has combined his considerable talents as a photographer, writer, poet and public speaker with his acute sense of needs in the marketplace to create a publishing company that today is recognised worldwide.

Steve's primary goal is to turn the world on to nature, and, in pursuit of this lifelong objective, he has published a world-class range of children's books and learning aids. He sees our children as the decision makers of tomorrow and the guardians of our heritage.

Published by Steve Parish Publishing Pty Ltd

PO Box 1058, Archerfield, Queensland 4108 Australia

© copyright Steve Parish Publishing Pty Ltd

ISBN 1 740218493

10 9 8 7 6 5 4 3 2 1

Photography: Steve Parish;

Additional Photography: p. 25 bottom, South Australian Museum.

Text: Karin Cox, SPP; Editing: Michele Perry, SPP; Kate Lovett; Design: Fanni Kosztolanyi.

Photos: Cover and pp. 4–5: the spires of St Peter's Cathedral in North Adelaide with city highrises beyond; p. 1: Sturt's Desert Pea; pp. 2–3: Adelaide city on the Torrens River.

Prepress by Colour Chiefs Digital Imaging, Australia

Printed in China by Printplus Limited

Produced in Australia at the Steve Parish Publishing Studios

Steve Parish
PUBLISHING

FOR PRODUCTS
www.steveparish.com.au

FOR LIMITED EDITION PRINTS
www.steveparishexhibits.com.au

FOR PHOTOGRAPHY EZINE
www.photographaustralia.com.au

online